TRIBAL CONSULTATION STRATEGIES FOR BEGINNERS, PART II

OUTLINE OF FEDERAL INDIAN LAW & POLICIES IN U.S. HISTORY

GEORGEIE REYNOLDS, PhD

INTRODUCTION

This is the second part in my Tribal consultation strategies series. The first one gave advice, guidance, & tips on how to interact with Tribes in a culturally sensitive way, & carry out a successful consultation meeting.

This booklet provides a brief history in bullet form of Federal Indian laws enacted throughout our history, Labels of the historic time periods are taken from Stephen Pevar (2012), an expert in this field, & a respected authority whose book you should read. See the bibliography on the last page.

Here's a piece of advice: Don't argue about statutes, regulations, & policies with a Tribal member, especially a Chairman or a lawyer—they likely know more about these things than you do because they *have* to know—their people are directly affected. Discussion may be fine, but arguing is not a path I'd choose.

Please email me questions, criticisms, or comments at archaeofun@gmail.com, or drop me a line at P O Box 3198, Portland OR 97208. We can start a dialogue & involve others who share our interests if you like.

I hope you will enjoy getting to know Tribal Nations. Working with Tribal governments is the most rewarding endeavor I can think of.

Best,

Georgeie Reynolds

Remember, it was all theirs!

COLONIAL PERIOD (TO 1789)

1492 & before:

- Indigenous people have occupied the "New World" for thousands of years.
- There may have been 12 million+ inhabitants (give or take), most with highly complex cultures.
- Belief systems were based on the inter-connection of all things – human beings, the land, rocks, water and animals. This belief is still widely held.
- Although the concept of land ownership was different, Tribes governed all lands.

After 1492:

- Conquerors included England, France, Spain, & Holland.
- Doctrine of Discovery:
  - Issued as Papal Bull by Pope Alexander VI in 1493.
  - Inhabitants may only occupy lands, not "own" them.
  - Conquering Nations have Divine Right to take lands through Treaty, purchase, or conquest.

EARLY U.S. POLICY

Tribes are considered sovereigns.

US Constitution (1789)

- Article I, Sec VIII: Commerce Clause—gives specific authority to Congress to regulate commerce with Tribes.
- Article VI: Treaty Clause—only President & Senate have authority to enter into a Treaty with a Tribe.

> The Constitution elevates the status of Indian Tribes as legal entities to the Federal level. State & local governments do not have jurisdiction.

> The downside for Tribes: Congress has "plenary" or complete power over Tribes. Congress can rescind Treaties or take away federal recognition.

Treaty-Making (1778-1871)

Recognized Tribal & US government as equal & sovereign.

- Addressed in US Constitution, Art. VI, above.
- More than 400 Treaties signed in 18th-19th centuries.
- Delaware Nation signed 1st Treaty in 1778.
- Most Treaties promised services and tracts of land in exchange for aboriginal territories.

- Treaty-making ended in 1871:
  - House of Representatives pressured Senate to cease Treaty-making.
  - Because the House wanted a say in Indian policy.
  - All agreements now done by legislation (House & Senate).
  - Legislation does not require a Tribe's consent.
  - Therefore, easier to take Indian land & status.
- Existing Treaties were upheld, but . . .
- . . . all Treaties have been violated to some degree (i.e., lands taken).

> **Fact:** The Bureau of Indian Affairs was founded in 1824 & placed in the War Department.

REMOVAL ERA (1820s-1850s)

This was a dismal time for Tribal Nations although it started with three pro-Indian landmark Supreme Court Cases commonly referred to as The Marshall Trilogy, named for Chief Justice John Marshall.

- **Johnson v McIntosh** (1823)
  -- Private citizens can't purchase lands from Indians.

- **Cherokee Nation v Georgia** (1831)
  -- States cannot enforce their laws on Tribes.
  -- Labeled Tribes "domestic dependent nations."[1]

- **Worcester v Georgia** (1832)
  -- Strengthened idea of Tribal sovereignty.
  -- Fed government has sole authority to interact with Tribes.
  -- State permits invalid for people to enter Tribal lands.

Bottom line: the Marshall Trilogy upheld Tribal sovereignty & held that only Congress could interact legally with Tribes, not state or local governments.

---

[1] While this case reinforced the legal standing of Tribes with the Federal government, the labeling of Tribes as "domestic dependent nations" has perpetuated the idea of a relationship of non-equals between Congress and Tribes.

REMOVAL ERA, continued

If Chief Justice Marshall was an advocate for Tribes, President Andrew Jackson was an adversary. Unhappy with the Marshall Trilogy, Jackson, the "Indian Fighter," is reported to have said, "Marshall has made his decision; now let him enforce it."

- As President (1829-1837), he began removal process.
- **Indian Removal Act** (1830) authorized President to negotiate removal of Indians to west of Mississippi due to population growth of settlers.
- Also a negative response to Marshall decisions upholding sovereignty & the Trust responsibility.
- Purpose of removal: separate Indians & non-Indians; grab Indian land for settlers.
- Southeastern & northeastern Tribes moved to Oklahoma & Midwest due to pressure for land by settlers.
- Some Tribes, i.e., Potawatomi, Delaware, moved several times.[2]

---

2 The Delaware Nation moved from Delaware to Ohio, Indiana, Missouri, and, finally, to Oklahoma.

Cherokee Removal, 1836-1839

-- Includes Trail of Tears—20,000[3] people died on way to Oklahoma, but this is just an estimate.

-- Southeastern Tribes affected: Cherokee, Chickasaw, Creek, Muskogee, Seminole, Choctaw, others.

-- Removed from: Georgia, Florida, Carolinas, Tennessee, Alabama, Texas.

-- Removed to Oklahoma (Indian Territory).

-- Voluntary at first, then forced, then violent.

-- Treaty of New Echota (1835): Tribes given $5 million in exchange for lands east of the Mississippi.

Do Tribes pay taxes? Yes, they pay Federal tax, but not state tax. They may also pay a reservation tax.

Do Tribes get handouts, like free education? No, they don't. The services they receive are "payment" for the lands they handed over to the Federal government through Treaties, Executive Orders, or legislation.

3 Very rough estimate; does not include all affected Tribes.

RESERVATION ERA (1850s-1880s)

- Further removal became difficult, so Tribes placed on reservations, most with a US Indian Agent.
- Lands lost as settlers moved into former territories.
- Tribes no longer considered independent sovereigns.
- Goals: convert to Christianity & assimilate.
- 300 reservations created, some containing large tracts of land.
- Boarding schools established beyond reservation boundaries to eliminate Indian cultural traditions—spiritual practices, languages, braids & long hair cut, traditional dances, etc.
- **Major Crimes Act** (1885):

  -- Gave Federal courts jurisdiction over major crimes committed by one Indian against another on reservations.

  -- Crimes included:
  Murder
  Rape
  Manslaughter
  Assault with intent to kill
  Arson
  Burglary
  Larceny

  -- Did away with pre-existing Tribal court systems.

What is a Federally recognized Tribe? A Tribe that has a legal relationship with the US government from a Treaty, Executive Order, or legislation. These Tribes, currently almost 570 in number, receive services, sometimes including monetary compensation, from the government. These services are not handouts.

What about non-recognized Tribes? They have no legal relationship with the government and receive no services or monetary compensation. Many were unfairly terminated in the 1950s-1960s. The task of getting Federal recognition back is onerous—expensive & lengthy. They are treated the same as "interested parties," or "the public" by the Federal government. Some Tribes are state recognized and may receive limited benefits. Many non-recognized Tribes are landless.

Word to the wise: Federally recognized or not, treat all Tribes with respect. They deserve it & their recognition may have been forfeited capriciously.

In 2008, then candidate Barack Obama was adopted by the Crow Nation & given the name "One Who Helps People Throughout the Land." He was the first President to visit the reservation.

ALLOTMENT & ASSIMILATION (1887-1934)

Government decides Tribes should be assimilated into mainstream society by breaking up familial ties & giving left over lands to settlers.

GENERAL ALLOTMENT ACT OF 1887 (DAWES ACT)

- Broke up reservations by giving allotments of 160 acres to heads of households & 80 acres to others.
- Remaining land, declared "excess" by Dept. of the Interior, went to US settlers.
- Tribes lost 90 million acres of land.
- Worse, not only was land lost, but also fragmented:
  -- Extended families
  -- Tribal governments
  -- Tribal religions & cultures
- Stressed the Western concept of individual ownership & minimized Tribal communal life.

> **Note:** Every time a major piece of legislation was enacted, indigenous people lost millions of acres of land.

REORGANIZATION (1934-1953)

Government decides Tribes should exist in perpetuity, using a western model for their governments.

INDIAN REORGANIZATION ACT OF 1934

- Also known as Wheeler-Howard Act.
- Tribes have right to have own constitutions.
  -- Subject to approval by Dept. of Interior.
  -- Non-Indian governmental pattern.
- Stopped land allotment.
- Returned some unsold surplus lands to Tribes.
- Two million+ acres returned.
- Provided framework for self-governance.
- Tribes organizing constitutions under this Act are called IRA Tribes.

Indian Claims Commission formed 1946. Allowed Tribes to sue for compensation for lands taken by the Federal government illegally (i.e., in violation of a Treaty).

TERMINATION & RELOCATION (1953-1967)

Government decides to assimilate Indians — incorporate them into the dominant culture.

BIA initiated a program to pay some Indians to relocate to urban areas such as New York, Chicago, and Denver.

- **House Concurrent Resolution 108 (1953)**

  -- Trust relationship with 109 Tribes terminated.

  -- Lands sold; Tribes subject to state laws.

- **Public Law 280 (1953)**

  -- Reservations in certain states subject to state civil & criminal jurisdictions.

  -- States in question seen as having Tribes that were troublemakers—CA, MN, NE, OR & WI. AK added in 1958.

  -- Did not completely extinguish Trust relationship, but greatly diminished it.

Indian land base at lowest: 50M acres.

Poverty rampant. Alcoholism at all-time high.

No college grads except for Cherokee & Choctaw.

SELF-DETERMINATION ERA (1968-?)

Tribes are given more autonomy

Indian Civil Rights Act (1968)—Portions of Bill of Rights guaranteed on Indian land even though Tribal members also under jurisdiction of Tribal courts.

Indian Self-Determination & Education Assistance Act (1975)—Gives Tribes almost total control over contracts & grants awarded to them by Federal government. Enables Tribes to set own agenda.

Indian Tribal Justice Support Act (1993) established office in BIA to support/develop Tribal justice systems. Provided funding, training, & technical support for the operation of Tribal courts & other parts of the justice system.

General Welfare Exclusion Act (2014) clarifies the treatment of general welfare benefits provided by Indian Tribes. Any welfare received from a Tribal government is not included in a Tribal member's gross income.

Indian Trust Asset Reform Act, 2016 reaffirms government's Trust responsibility; tribes submit to DOI Indian trust asset management plans for possible implementation.

When did Indians get the right to vote?: In 1924, with the passage of the Indian Citizenship Act (Snyder Act). But, because states controlled the vote, some states were later, with New Mexico being the last, 1962.

WHAT'S NEXT

As of September 30, 2017, this is the status of the following major pieces of legislation designed to help Indian Country.

Native American Energy Act (HR 210): to facilitate energy development on Indian lands.
Most recent action: Referred to House Subcommittee on Indians, Insular & Alaska Native Affairs, 2/10/17.

Indian Health Care Improvement Act (HR 1369)—up for reauthorization. Governs management of Indian health by the Indian Health Service. Provides for care & education by IHS of Federally recognized Tribes.
Most recent action: Introduced 3/6/17.

Tribal Labor Sovereignty Act (HR 968) removes National Labor Relations Board jurisdiction from Indian businesses located on Indian reservations.
Most recent action: Reported out of the House Education & Workforce Committee, 6/29/17

United Nations Declaration of the Rights of Indigenous Peoples (UNDRIP) adopted 2007. Australia, UK, US & Canada (all former colonies of the UK with major indigenous populations) voted against. Obama stated US would lend support to UNDRIP in 2010, but Congress must approve. Recognizes right of all indigenous peoples to self-governance. As a UN declaration, UNDRIP is not legally binding.

A WORD ABOUT ALASKA NATIVES AND NATIVE HAWAIIANS

With the passage of the Alaska Native Claims Settlement Act (1971), most **Alaskan villages** became the of equivalent of Federally recognized Tribes when Village Corporations and Regional Corporations were formed. Alaska Natives could choose 4,000,000 acres of lands in the ensuing years, but all future land claims were extinguished.

Native Hawaiians are not Federally recognized Tribes & are represented by the Office of Hawaiian Affairs, founded in 1978. The Trust Responsibility does not exist in Hawaii, BIA has no presence, & Native Hawaiians do not receive government services. Legislation has been introduced by the Hawai'ian congressional delegation over the past few sessions of Congress to change the status of Native Hawaiians, but has not yet been successful.

REMEMBER THESE THREE PRINCIPLES OF FEDERAL INDIAN LAW

TRUST RESPONSIBILITY—the concept that the US Federal government has a fiduciary responsibility to federally recognized Tribes to provide goods & services in exchange for lands given surrendered. It applies to individuals as well as Tribes.

SOVEREIGNTY—Tribes are independent governmental entities, distinct from federal, state, & local governments . . .

GOVERNMENT-TO-GOVERNMENT RELATIONSHIPS . . Tribes must be treated as governmental entities, with whom we have a legally binding relationship as equals.

To these, I'd like to add self-determination, although this forward-looking doctrine does not have a long history. Let's hope it's on the books for good.

SELF-DETERMINATION—Tribes have the ability to decide their own fate & future despite the plenary power of Congress.

Fact: In order to receive Federal services such as health care, Indians must carry an identity card to prove their enrollment in a Federally recognized Tribe.

SUGGESTED READING

Canby, William C., Jr.
1998 *American Indian Law in a Nutshell.*
St. Paul: West Group.

Echo Hawk, Walter R.
2010 *In the Courts of the Conqueror: The 10 Worst Indian Law Cases Ever Decided.*
Golden , CO: Fulcrum Publishing

Keown, Larry D.
2010 Working in Indian Country.
Austin TX: Hugo House Publishers, Ltd

Mann, Charles C.
2006 *1492: New Revelations of the Americas Before Columbus.* New York: Vintage Press.

Pevar, Stephen L.
2012 *The Rights of Indians & Tribes: The Authoritative ACLU Guide to Indian & Tribal Rights.*
New York: Oxford University Press.

———

2010 *The Declaration of Independence & The Constitution of the United States*. New York: Bantam Press.

Notes

Notes

Made in the USA
Monee, IL
09 November 2026

67972906R00017